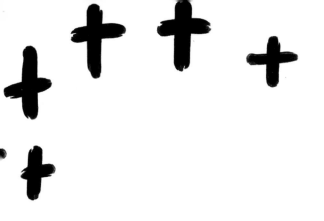

This book belongs to

_____

10 WAYS TO FALL IN LOVE WITH YOUR BIBLE

AND STAY IN LOVE

SHANNA NOEL

DaySpring

LIVE YOUR FAITH

Table of Contents

Introduction

Hiya, friend!

Can we just start off with a little honesty?

I haven't always loved my Bible.

Now, I know what you're probably thinking. (Go ahead and check the cover; yep, you're still in the right place.) And, maybe this sort of confession isn't exactly the right way to start a book like this. But, hey, I didn't want to jump into this thing without being 100 percent honest with you. So here's the unvarnished truth: for most of my walk, I struggled to read my Bible, struggled to understand my Bible, struggled to learn from my Bible, and, most importantly, struggled to love my Bible. For most of my Christian journey, I've had trouble carving out a few minutes each day to spend in God's Word, and when I did manage to find the time, my eyes often glazed over.

As a pastor's wife, I felt no small amount of guilt. I thought I was supposed to know more details, to memorize more verses, to understand more history, and to have informed opinions on everything from Genesis to Revelation. So, why, I asked myself, was it so hard for me to read and study the Bible? Maybe I just needed a better Bible, one with better notes, nicer fonts, and prettier pictures. I convinced myself that when I found the "perfect" Bible, everything might change, so I kept searching for the right one.

My dream Bible was the perfect translation, the perfect size, the perfect weight, with the perfect cover and perfectly sized print. I thought—wrongly—that if I finally found the right Bible, I might finally get serious about reading it. Of course, that plan always backfired. Every time I bought a new "perfect" Bible, it just ended up gathering more dust on the already-dusty shelf alongside all the other dust-covered "perfect" Bibles that I had already bought, but not read. The result? Even more guilt!

Gradually, I fell further and further into an unfortunate cycle: the more I avoided God's Word, the guiltier I felt; and the guiltier I felt, the more I avoided it. For me, the Bible had become a source of stress rather than a beautiful gift.

In an effort to assuage my guilt, I began each new year with the very same goal: to read the Bible from cover to cover. And, on New Year's Day, I usually started strong. I'd find a quiet spot, set aside ten minutes, and bingo! One day down, and only 364 to go. Day two? The same. Day three? Still on track. Usually, I managed to stay the course for a week, maybe two, but it didn't last, and by the third week in January, I'd be hopelessly behind. Oh, well, I'd tell myself: there's always next year.

My Bible-reading reluctance stemmed from the mistaken belief that if I found the right translation, or the right font, or the right read-the-Bible-in-a-year plan, I'd finally fall in love with God's Word. I was looking for a key to unlock God's gift, but there is no key, no secret, no hack to decode and understand His Word. He is the only key we need in life.

For me, everything changed when I stopped viewing the Bible as a source of guilt and began viewing it as a gift. I needed to hand the whole matter over to Him. Instead of running from Christ, I needed to run *to* Him, to ask Him to help me understand. And I needed to leave all that guilt at the cross.

I also needed to abandon the worldly expectations of what reading the Bible should look like and allow Him to walk me through the Word in a personal and meaningful way. In the following chapters, I want you to keep this journey in mind. I encourage you to use this book as a tool to better understand ways to approach the Bible. I've included some practical ideas that have helped me, and I pray that they'll help you. But until you surrender this journey to Christ, I'm afraid you will only find yourself back at square one.

Five years ago, I was at square one. If you had told me then that I would write a book about loving the Bible, I would have laughed. I would have said to myself, "Nope, that's not me. Somebody else will need to write *that* book!" But a lot has changed in the last five years. After spending too many years avoiding my Bible, I finally fell in love with it. And you can too.

Today, I don't have all the answers; I don't have it all figured out; I haven't memorized all the verses; and I still can't pronounce all the names. But I can tell you I am learning daily about His beautiful gift, and I can tell you that I'm so thankful to have fallen head over heels in love with His Word.

Now may the God
of hope fill you with
all joy and peace
in believing,
so that you may
overflow with hope
by the power
of the Holy Spirit.

ROMANS 15:13 HCSB

#1
Get Rid of the Excuses

"The pathway to freedom begins when we face the problem without making excuses for it."

JOYCE MEYER

Let's get things started by talking about all those pesky excuses. You know the ones I'm referring to: all those hypothetical reasons that we conjure up in order to convince ourselves we simply don't have time to read our Bibles. I know most of the excuses because I've used them myself, on too many occasions to count. Here are a few of my greatest hits:

"There aren't enough hours in the day."
"Mornings are too busy and at night, I'm too exhausted."
"My (fill in the blank) takes up all my free time."
"It's too noisy around here. I can't concentrate."
"I'll get around to it someday."

Excuses like these are troublesome because each of them contains a grain of truth. Yes, most of us are busy.

And yes, we do have responsibilities that occupy our time and sap our strength. We have jobs, families, and friends; we belong to churches and civic organizations; we do housework, charity work, yardwork, and sometimes we even help with the kids' homework. We're caring for all sorts of people: little ones, big ones, young ones, old ones, and just about every age bracket in between. All those people—plus all the other responsibilities—are vying for our attention and our time.

And, yes, we do live in a noisy, interconnected world filled with enough distractions to sidetrack even the most saintly among us. Sure, we've all heard stories about those amazing Christian women who get up every morning at 4:00 a.m. and read their Bibles for an hour and a half. But what about the rest of us? What about those of us who are barely getting by with too little sleep, too many responsibilities, and not enough caffeine? Can I get an amen?

And what about our good intentions? Don't they count for something?

Before I fell in love with my Bible, I had all the good intentions a pastor's wife could ask for. I intended to become a serious student of my Bible *someday* (but not *this* day). I intended to read God's Word carefully, and talk to Him frequently at some point in the not-too-distant future (with emphasis on the words *distant* and *future*). Those were my intentions. They were real intentions, honest intentions, well-meaning intentions. But my excuses kept getting in the way.

Not that I didn't try.

I really *wanted* to read my Bible and soak in all that wisdom. I knew that God's Book was loaded with eternal truths, and I knew that God's Son was speaking to me across the millennia, sharing His message of hope and assurance. But for some reason, the whole process of picking up my Bible and reading it every day seemed more like an obligation than an opportunity. So I invented a string of excuses—spoken mostly to myself—that created short-term justification for my inaction. In the long term, however, the excuses led to procrastination and procrastination led to guilt.

Now, I realize that I was waiting for the perfect conditions to fulfill my "obligation" to God. I wanted to have the perfect Bible, the perfect setting, the perfect amount of time, and the perfect attitude before I got serious. So if you, like me, have some perfectionistic tendencies, here's my word of warning: there's never a perfect time to start anything.

If you wait for perfect conditions, you will never get anything done.

ECCLESIASTES 11:4 TLB

I Will Wait until I Can Do It Just Right!

"The person who waits until circumstances completely favor his undertaking will never accomplish anything."

MARTIN LUTHER

It's been said in many different ways on many different occasions, but get ready because I'm about to say it again: perfectionism is the enemy of progress. There, I said it. But do you really believe it? I hope so, because it's true. If you're hanging out, biding your time, waiting for just the right moment and just the right conditions to begin your spiritual journey—or any other kind of journey, for that matter—you'll be waiting for a very long time.

And the longer you wait, the more things you'll miss as the hours, days, weeks, months, and years pass you by.

Perhaps you believe that this is the absolute *wrong* time to fall in love with your Bible. Maybe you're busier than you've ever been in your life. Perhaps you have too many items on your to-do list and too few hours in the day to do them. Or maybe you don't think you have what it takes to be a true spiritual pilgrim right now. Maybe you're waiting for a time when you feel closer to God. Or maybe, just maybe, you're waiting for some sort of sign. Well, if that's what you're waiting for, consider this book your sign. Why? Because no matter your circumstances, no matter your obligations, no matter your resources or lack thereof, the best day to fall in love with your Bible is today.

Not tomorrow.

Not next week, next month, or next year.

When it comes to your unfolding relationship with God, it's all about the present tense.

God isn't asking for your perfection; He's asking for your participation.

Think about it: if the Lord weeded out all the imperfect people in His church, who'd be left? The answer, of course, is nobody. All of us make mistakes, and we all fall short of the mark from time to time. So, if one of your excuses is, "I want to wait until I can do it *just right*," it's time to consider what you're waiting for and why.

Is next year *really* going to be the "perfect" time to get serious about your Bible? What about the year after that? In a year or two or three, will you really have, for the very first time in your life, all the time in the world to get closer to your Creator? Probably not. Every stage of life has its challenges, just as every stage of life has its opportunities. Next year's excuses may vary slightly from this year's excuses, but they'll still be excuses. And they'll still be major roadblocks on the path to spiritual growth.

"The one word in the spiritual vocabulary is NOW."

OSWALD CHAMBERS

Excuses are barriers that we all face from time to time. So what can we do to move beyond them? First, we must acknowledge that they do, indeed, carry a grain of truth, but not the whole truth. Then, we must disown them. How? By turning them over to God.

When we turn our concerns over to the Lord, He will build a path through the wilderness. When we release our troubles to Him, He will provide the tools we need to move beyond every dilemma, every difficulty, every predicament, and every excuse. The things that we can't do alone, we can do with Him.

But prove yourselves
doers of the word,
and not merely hearers
who delude themselves.

JAMES 1:22 NASB

Priorities

"Your choices and decisions are a reflection of how well you've set and followed your priorities."
ELIZABETH GEORGE

From the moment you open your eyes in the morning until the moment you close them and drift off to sleep at night, the world is vying for your attention. Think about how much screen time you spend on an average day. Think about all the people, all the organizations, and all the responsibilities that keep you charging from place to place, trying to get it all done. If you're like me, you get tired just thinking about it. That's why we need a few clearly stated priorities. If you don't prioritize your day and your life, the world will simply gobble up every spare minute, leaving you no time for God. And that's bad. Very bad.

The only way you're going to fall in love with your Bible is to make it a top priority. Not your only priority, but a top-tier, get-it-done priority that automatically appears on your to-do list every day. I'm not telling you to get up every morning at 4:00 a.m. I'm not even telling you that Bible reading needs to be a morning ritual. Maybe afternoons or evenings work better for you. If so, go for it. But what I am telling you is this: unless you lose the excuses and make God a high priority, you might as well put this book down, clean off the smudge marks, and try to return it to your local bookstore. Why? Because this plan simply won't work if you can't, on an average day, manage to spend *any* time talking to your heavenly Father or reading the book He wrote.

Every day has 1,440 minutes. Subtract 480 of those

minutes for sleep (my math says that's eight hours, but I did it in my head, so you may want to check it out for yourself). You still have 960 minutes left. Subtract 480 minutes for work, and you *still* have 480 minutes left. Take a measly 5 percent of that free time, and you've got twenty-four minutes, which is about the length of an average thirty-minute TV show minus the commercials. Does twenty-four minutes sound like an eternity? How about ten? If you read your Bible for just ten minutes a day, that's only about 2 percent of your free time!

By the way, there's no law that says you can't keep up a running conversation with God throughout the day. I do. I try to spend a few minutes reading the Word in the morning, and then, for the remainder of the day, I talk to Him about the things I read and the things that are happening around me. The more I talk to Him, the more our relationship grows, the more blessings I manage to spot, and the more joy I feel in my heart.

So, let's get this out on the table right now: if you're ready to make God a priority, you're ready to take the next giant step in your spiritual journey. But unless you're willing to make Him a priority—unless you're willing to give Him a few percentage points of your free time each day—those same old, threadbare excuses will win every time.

> "When you live in the light of eternity, your values change."
>
> RICK WARREN

So let us stop
going over
the basic teachings
about Christ
again and again.
Let us go on instead
and become mature
in our understanding.

HEBREWS 6:1 NLT

Leave inexperience behind,
and you will live;
pursue the way
of understanding.

PROVERBS 9:6 HCSB

Bible Reading Can Be Habit-Forming

"We first make our habits, then our habits make us."
JOHN DRYDEN

As far as I'm concerned, habits come in two flavors: good and bad. The good habits make us healthier, happier, stronger, and smarter. Plus, the good habits tend to keep us on the spiritual path that God has chosen for us.

Bad habits do the opposite. They sap our strength, waste our time, deplete our resources, and send us down countless spiritual dead ends.

So, our challenge is clear: we must try, as best as we can, to increase the quantity and quality of our good habits and decrease the number and impact of the bad ones.

I don't have any scientific evidence to back me up, but I've found through personal experience that one good habit leads to another. By establishing one very good habit—reading the Bible every day—I've found that it's easier to focus on the good and to deflect the bad. I'm not saying that a ten-minute, once-a-day tour through your Bible will solve all your problems, but I am saying that it will help.

It has been said that habits are the fabric of life, and that's probably not much of an exaggeration. We human beings are, indeed, creatures of habit. That's why it's so important to select our habits on purpose, not by accident. And no habit is more important than spending time each day with God.

All habits have a beginning point, and they all come with an expiration date. If you've picked up a few bad habits along this twisting, turning path called life, don't panic, don't beat yourself up, and don't feel like the Lone Ranger. Everybody has her own troublesome assortment of unfortunate habits, some of which may have started long ago and far away. But please remember this: no problem is too big for God, not even yours. And the best way to start offloading bad habits and replacing them with better ones is to form the foundational habit of spending a few minutes every day with Him.

+ + + + + + + + +

"We must exchange the philosophy of excuse— what I am is beyond my control— for the philosophy of personal responsibility."

BARBARA JORDAN

+ + + + + + + + +

Lose the Excuses Now

"NOW is the operative word.
Everything you put in your way
is just a method of putting off the hour
when you could actually be doing your dream.
You don't need endless time
and perfect conditions. Do it now."
BARBARA SHER

When it comes to falling in love with our Bibles, absence does *not* make the heart grow fonder. We can't just *talk* about reading the Bible; we can't *intend* to read it; we can't *plan* on reading it; we can't *hope* that we'll eventually get around to reading it. We've got to pick it up, open it to a particular page, and actually start *reading* it. Period.

The road to apathy is paved with good intentions. Yet a thousand good intentions pale in comparison to a single positive accomplishment. Excuses are the enemy because many of the things we put off until tomorrow never get done. Excuses are simply the strategy that we subconsciously employ to postpone the things that we assume will be unpleasant, unhelpful, or just plain boring.

So, step number one is ridding yourself of every excuse you've used to avoid an intimate relationship with God's Word. Vanquish those excuses once and for all. When you do, you're on your way!

Your Personal Top 5: Excuses

Try to think of five excuses you've used to avoid regular daily Bible reading. Jot them down below.

1. _____

2. _____

3. _____

4. _____

5. _____

Finishing is better than starting. Patience is better than pride.

ECCLESIASTES 7:8 NLT

Your Personal Top 10: Priorities

On the lines below, make a list of ten things that are high priorities for you. By the way, is your relationship with God on that list?

1. _____

2. _____

3. _____

4. _____

5. _____

6. _____

7. _____

8. _____

9. _____

10. _____

Therefore, with your minds ready for action,
be serious and set your hope completely on the grace
to be brought to you at the revelation of Jesus Christ.
I PETER 1:13 HCSB

When you make a vow to God, do not delay to fulfill it.
ECCLESIASTES 5:4 NIV

Therefore, whether you eat or drink,
or whatever you do, do everything for God's glory.
I CORINTHIANS 10:31 HCSB

Now, Lord, what do I wait for? My hope is in You.
PSALM 39:7 HCSB

#2

Turn the Guilt into a Gift

*"Regret is an appalling waste of energy;
you can't build on it. It's only good for wallowing in."*
KATHERINE MANSFIELD

Once you've confronted all those timeworn excuses for not reading your Bible—and once you've removed them from your internal phrasebook—spend some time thinking about guilt. Maybe you have zero guilt about the ways you've been reading and treating your Bible. If so, congratulations. But if you're like the rest of us, you probably feel a few pangs of regret about the way you've been relating to the book that God wrote. I experienced low-grade guilt for years. In fact, the Bible became a nagging source of guilt for me. Let me explain.

For many years, I felt that I "should" approach God's Word in a certain, prescribed, socially acceptable way. First, I convinced myself that unless I could spend big blocks of time reading it every day (which was almost impossible for me), I was damaged goods. Next, I felt that the notes I made in my Bible should look a certain way (prim, proper, black-and-white notations in the margin were okay, but colorful comments and drawings were out of bounds). And since I knew my Bible was a very special book, I convinced myself that it must be treated with kid gloves. So I took great pains to ensure that it stayed in tip-top shape, with no dog-eared pages, no crinkled covers, and no coffee stains.

But the word of the Lord endures forever. And this is the word that was preached as the gospel to you.

I PETER 1:25 HCSB

The good news? All my Bibles were in near-mint condition.

The bad news? I didn't read them very much. So I didn't experience the full measure of joy that comes from an intimate love-relationship with the Word.

To make matters worse, I felt the additional responsibility of being a pastor's wife. Shouldn't I be one of the most biblically literate people in our congregation? Shouldn't I know every nook and cranny of the New Testament *and* the Old? Shouldn't I know all the names and all the stories?

And shouldn't I be able to recite the perfect verse at the perfect moment to make a perfectly timed contribution to any conversation? Well, shouldn't I?

Without realizing it, I had bound myself up with so

many "shoulds"—so many things that I "had to do" before getting in touch with God's message—that I turned Bible reading into a chore. No wonder I avoided it! I had mistakenly contaminated God's gift with my own self-generated feelings of guilt. My guilty conscience was constructing a psychological barrier between God's Word and my heart.

As for God,

His way is perfect;

the word of the Lord is proven;

He is a shield to all

who trust in Him.

PSALM 18:30 NKJV

Guilt: A Guiding Light or a Spiritual Dead End?

"The purpose of guilt is to bring us to Jesus. Once we are there, then its purpose is finished."
CORRIE TEN BOOM

Sometimes, guilt serves a positive purpose. When we feel genuine regret for our mistakes—when we turn away from destructive behaviors and turn back to God—our feelings of remorse are helpful. In such cases, our guilty feelings serve as warning messages from above. You can think of these emotions as the check-engine light of your soul. When God speaks to you in the quiet corners of your conscience—when that little red light turns on in your brain, telling you that something bad might be about to happen—you'd best check things out with your Creator. When God speaks to your heart, you must listen. Carefully.

But there's another type of guilt that's definitely *not* helpful: irrational guilt. It's what Erma Bombeck was talking about when she said, "Guilt is the gift that keeps on giving." Irrational guilt consists of a series of self-generated messages that convince you—wrongly—that you're a horrible person (when you're not), that some activity is a surefire sin (when it isn't), or that certain things must be done in a specific, "socially acceptable" way (when logic dictates otherwise).

In my own case, the guilt I felt concerning my Bible was illogical and self-defeating. By convincing myself that I had to study the Word in a certain way, and that my Bible needed to be maintained in pristine, like-new condition, I was missing the point. In truth, God didn't

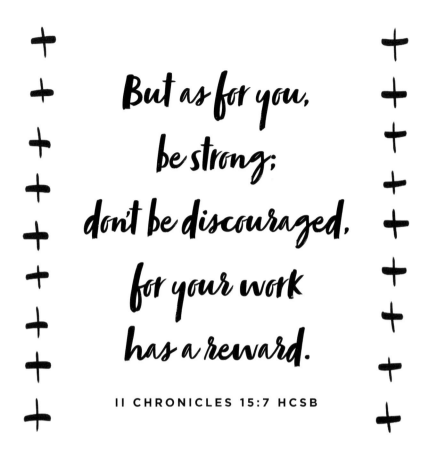

But as for you,
be strong;
don't be discouraged,
for your work
has a reward.

II CHRONICLES 15:7 HCSB

care what my Bible looked like, just as long as I used it. And He didn't demand that I spend hours every day on my knees—or that I know every name, story, and verse—in order to have a genuine relationship with Him.

I had been caught in a trap of my own making, a web of subtle guilty feelings that caused me, time and again, to put distance between myself and God's Word. Sometimes, I spent more brain power *avoiding* the Bible than *reading* it.

Then one day, I came across a quote that changed all that.

Therefore, if anyone is in Christ, he is a new creation; old things have passed away; behold, all things have become new.

II CORINTHIANS 5:17 NKJV

Falling Apart?

*"A Bible that's falling apart
usually belongs to someone who isn't."*
C. H. SPURGEON

Sometimes, a single good idea can totally rearrange your thoughts and redirect your life. That's exactly what happened to me when I read C. H. Spurgeon's quote about a Bible that's falling apart. When I read those words and thought about what they meant, something clicked. That single sentence gave me a fresh perspective because it forced me to reconsider the way I'd been approaching God's Word.

First, I had to face the fact that my own Bibles were certainly *not* falling apart. In fact, most of them were in pristine condition.

Next, I decided that my collection of like-new Bibles (on the shelf) weren't doing me, or anybody else, much good. That's when I decided to take a different approach. I decided to take off the kid gloves and begin treating my Bible as a gift, not as a source of guilt. And I accepted the fact that if I really loved God's Word, I'd treat it like a familiar tool, not a museum piece. No more "perfect" Bibles parked quietly on the bookshelf. Instead, I wanted one Bible that I used until it finally fell apart. Literally.

I'm a visual learner. I like bright colors, pithy sayings, cute sketches, crazy fonts, and scrapbooks. So I decided that the best way to initiate my new read-and-understand-the-Bible strategy was to make colorful notes in the margin, complete with an assortment of personal glyphs and sketches. If this Bible was going to be mine, really mine, it needed to reflect my own style.

So I took my journaling Bible over to the scrapbooking table and got busy. I grabbed my notes from a recent sermon and began converting them into illustrated messages that I wanted to store in my permanent memory bank. Know what? It worked. Instantly. The minute I began adding my own color-coordinated illustrations and notations, my Bible-reluctance disappeared. Suddenly, I was experiencing more joy, more excitement, more fun, more meaning, and zero guilt. But I still wasn't sure that my newly found form of worship was right for other people, and I was concerned how others might react. So I didn't tell anybody, at least not at first. But God put a whisper in my heart, and I sensed that I needed to share my Bible-study experiment with others. Gradually, I began blogging about my experiences. Soon, I discovered that what worked for me worked for other women too. Thus began an endeavor called Illustrated Faith, a project that has turned from a part-time avocation into a growing, worldwide community.

> *I remind you to fan into flames the spiritual gift God gave you.*
>
> II TIMOTHY 1:6 NLT

The quotation that started it all proved true for me. Once my Bible started falling apart, many things started falling into place. And I'm confident that the same will hold true for you and your loved ones. As your Bible starts to fall apart from constant use, things will start falling together *for you*.

"Read the Bible
as though it
had not been set before
you ready-made.
Face the book with
a new attitude
as something new."

MARTIN BUBER

Guilt? No!
Gift? Yes!

"God's Book is packed with overwhelming riches.
They are unsearchable—the more we have,
the more there is to have."
OSWALD CHAMBERS

The Bible is not a traditional book. In fact, it's so different from other books that it deserves to be in its own category: the "heavenly gifts" category.

God's Word is a priceless blessing from our Creator, a tool that He intends for us to use in every aspect of our lives. The Bible contains promises that we all can depend on, whatever our circumstances. If we find ourselves standing on one of life's mountaintops, we need the Bible. If we're trudging through one of life's inevitable valleys, we need the Bible. And if we find ourselves stuck somewhere in between, we still need the Bible. Whether we're six, sixty, or 106, we need the Bible. But we don't have to be Bible scholars to understand it. We don't have to be perfect Christians, reading perfect Bibles, understanding everything perfectly. We simply need to open God's Book and be open to His guidance. When we do, He'll show us the way— His way—and we'll be blessed by His gift just as surely as we've been transformed forever by the sacrifice of His Son.

Your Bible contains powerful prescriptions for everyday living. It contains promises that can inspire you and reassure you. When you're discouraged, God's Word can give you hope. When you're depressed, God's Word can give you encouragement. When you're searching for meaning, God's Word will help you find it. When you're ready to celebrate life, God's Word will encourage you to rejoice.

The Holy Bible is, indeed, a priceless, one-of-a-kind gift from the Creator. Treat it that way. And read it that way.

> "The Reference Point for the Christian is the Bible. All values, judgments, and attitudes must be gauged in relationship to this Reference Point."
>
> **RUTH BELL GRAHAM**

(Almost) No Regrets

"Don't waste energy regretting the way things are
or thinking about what might have been.
Start at the present moment—accepting things
exactly as they are—and search for My way
in the midst of those circumstances."
SARAH YOUNG

When people ask me if I have any regrets about my own personal relationship with God's Word, I admit that I have only one: I regret that I didn't fall in love with the Bible sooner. I know that my life would have been richer had I done so, and I'll always wonder what spiritual treasures I might have discovered along the way.

But when it comes to regrets, I think less is more. So I don't focus on them. And neither should you.

In Isaiah 43, we read: "The Lord says, 'Forget what happened before, and do not think about the past. Look at the new thing I am going to do. It is already happening. Don't you see it? I will make a road in the desert and rivers in the dry land'" (v. 18–19 NCV). That's solid advice. Don't focus so intently on the rearview mirror that you take your eyes off the main highway. Just open your heart to God, listen

Your word is a lamp for my feet and a light on my path.

PSALM 119:105 HCSB

carefully to the messages He places on your heart, and leave the rest up to Him.

The correct moment to fall in love with your Bible is the present moment (if not sooner!). From personal experience, I can assure you that there's no reason for delay. The sooner you accept God's gift, the sooner you'll extinguish any nagging guilty feelings that may have been holding you back. And the sooner His blessings will begin to flow from that incredible gift, His Holy Word.

The LORD says, "I will guide you along the best pathway for your life. I will advise you and watch over you."

PSALM 32:8 NLT

Your Personal Top 5: Guilt

Try to think of five ways that you've allowed irrational guilt to interfere with your personal or spiritual growth. Write them down in the space below.

1. _____

2. _____

3. _____

4. _____

5. _____

Thanks be to God for His indescribable gift.

II CORINTHIANS 9:15 HCSB

Your Personal Top 10:
God's Gifts to You and Yours

On the lines below, make a list of ten ways that God has blessed you and yours. By the way, is the Bible included on that list?

1. _____

2. _____

3. _____

4. _____

5. _____

6. _____

7. _____

8. _____

9. _____

10. _____

Man shall not live by bread alone,
but by every word that proceeds
from the mouth of God.
MATTHEW 4:4 NKJV

For the word of God is living and effective
and sharper than any double-edged sword,
penetrating as far as the separation
of soul and spirit, joints and marrow.
It is able to judge the ideas and thoughts of the heart.
HEBREWS 4:12 HCSB

Anyone who listens to my teaching
and follows it is wise,
like a person who builds a house on solid rock.
Though the rain comes in torrents
and the floodwaters rise
and the winds beat against that house,
it won't collapse because it is built on bedrock.
MATTHEW 7:24-25 NLT

#3

Get Personal

"The Bible grows more beautiful as we grow in our understanding of it."

JOHANN WOLFGANG VON GOETHE

Now comes the fun part: let's talk about ways to personalize your Bible.

When you stop to think about it, people have been personalizing Bibles for years—but on a much smaller scale—by embossing their names on the front. Now, I'd like you to consider taking a giant leap forward. I'd like you to consider—and pray about—*really* personalizing your Bible, complete with colorful notes, happy quotes, memorable memos, and vivid illustrations. I can't promise that this style will work for you, but I do know that it has worked for me. And there's a reason.

I'm one of those visual people who retains information better when it's presented in living color. I find it easier to remember things when they're "chunked" in small, concise, easy-to-understand formats. And when I encounter things that are meaningful to me, I feel the urge to scrapbook them for future reference. So it's not surprising that, as a creative person, I find it easier to get excited about God's Word when I allow Him to help me bring His message to life through colors and illustrations. It's such a gift to walk with Him in this way. And I've been gratified to learn how many women feel the same way.

Before I began illustrating my Bible, studying God's Word was work. Hard work. Spending time in the Word was more like talking to a stranger than a best friend. Back in those days, my quiet moments with God were more formal, more distant, and more detached. But when I began illustrating my Bible, things changed. Now, when I pick up the Word, it's like talking to an old friend. Whether I've been away for an hour or a day, I can pick up right where I left off. My relationship to God's Word is more comfortable, more intimate, more relaxed, and, most importantly, more meaningful.

"God's Word is exciting, so electric, so energizing."

ELIZABETH GEORGE

And there's another benefit: now, when I have a spare minute or two, I'm actually *excited* to reach for my Bible and reconnect with God's message. I've found that meaningful moments don't always come at the end of a lengthy Bible reading. Sometimes, reading a single verse is enough to refocus my thoughts and redirect my day.

Of course, you'll have your own unique experiences as you illustrate your personal walk through God's Word. One of the great things about illustrating your Bible is that you'll have a tangible record of the thoughts and promises that brought meaning to your journey. In a very real sense, your personalized Bible becomes an illustrated *history* of your faith journey.

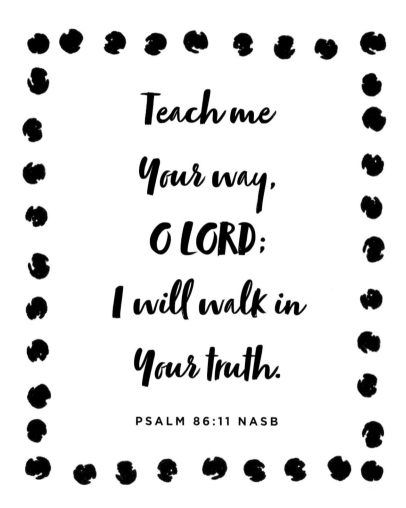

Teach me
Your way,
O LORD;
I will walk in
Your truth.

PSALM 86:11 NASB

Choosing a Bible That's Right for You

When it comes to choosing a Bible to claim as your own personalized version, there are no hard-and-fast rules except one: you need a Bible that's right for you. Do you love the King James Version? Go for it. Do you like one of the newer translations? Pick the one you like best. Do you already have a Bible that you love? That's wonderful! But if you're considering the purchase of a new Bible, I'd like to put in a plug for one of those wide-margined journaling Bibles that can be found at your friendly neighborhood Christian bookseller. These Bibles provide extra space for note-taking, and they come in almost every translation you can think of.

A wide-margin Bible gives you plenty of room to make notes and create illustrations. And some of the versions have slightly thicker paper that resists, but may not completely eliminate, bleed-through from one side of the page to another. That's why you may also want to consider an interleaved Bible, which has extra blank sheets between the pages of text. It's like having your very own drawing board within the covers of God's Word.

An interleaved Bible gives you the extra real estate you need to get creative, but there's a trade-off (isn't there always?).

With the extra pages comes extra weight and bulk. So, I currently leave my interleaved Bible at home and use a lighter, handier wide-margin journaling Bible for church, travel, and everyday use.

If you haven't yet discovered a translation that's absolutely, positively right for you, here's my recommendation: don't spend too much time worrying

"Get into the habit of dealing with God about everything."

OSWALD CHAMBERS

about it. And don't get caught up in a specific translation just because your grandmother likes it. Instead, keep looking around, and talk to your friends. Of course, you can always go online and compare translations whenever you've got a spare minute.

Selecting the right Bible is an important decision, and because it is important, I recommend that you pray about it. There are no questions too small, or too insignificant, for God. And when it comes to your journey through His Word, details matter. So whether you're sticking with a Bible that you've owned for years or selecting a new one from the bookstore shelf, give it lots of thought and lots of prayer.

Art Supplies

"Each one of us is God's special work of art."
JONI EARECKSON TADA

As the illustrator-in-chief of your own personalized Bible, you get to choose the tools you'll use to express yourself and document your faith. You may decide to start simply, with a few colored pencils and pens. Or you may go to the arts-and-crafts store and come home with a basketful of goodies. If you're a professional artist, you probably already have everything you need. If you're a total rookie, you may want to order a Bible-journaling starter kit from a Christian bookseller.

Here are a few of the supplies that will come in handy as you jump-start your illustrations:

- A devotional booklet (as an idea-starter)
- Sheets of cardstock stickers (wordfetti, flags, tabs, alphabets, shapes, etc.)
- A precision pen
- A good tape dispenser
- Acrylic paints (if you like to paint)
- Your favorite pens and colored pencils
- A small ink-proof mat or cutting pad (to make sure you don't slice the dining-room table or ink the tablecloth)
- And finally, a box to keep everything in

Getting Started

Let's say you've picked out the right Bible, accumulated the necessary supplies, and you're ready to begin illustrating your faith. How do you get started? Here's what I suggest:

- Spend time with God (read a devo; listen to worship music).
- Pray about it (ask God to guide you; pray, create, repeat).
- Write it down (what is God telling you?).
- Draw it (bring the big idea into the margins of your Bible).
- Date it (it's so important to date your entries because you're going to keep going back to these verses over and over).
- Tab it (use tabs to see what verses you're on).
- Forget the rules (just connect with God in the way that's most natural for you).

"Mark it down—
your progress
in holiness will
never exceed
your relationship
with the holy
Word of God."

NANCY LEIGH DEMOSS

Connect with God in Your Own Way

What I'm about to say is something you've undoubtedly heard before. And if you tell me it's trite, I'll say you're right. But you'll also have to admit that it's true. So here goes:

There's absolutely, positively nobody in the history of the universe who's exactly like you.

Nobody.

You're one of a kind.

You're the only you who's ever been and the only you who ever will be.

And since you are a unique creation, loved by God and gifted with special talents and opportunities, the worship style that fits others may not fit you. That's why I tell people to forget the rules and connect with God's Word in the way that feels most natural to them. As you worship the Lord and express your devotion to Him, feel free to draw outside the lines . . . or not.

If you're a person who simply wants to keep a journal outside your Bible, then you need nothing more than a pen and paper. If that's your style, start-up is simple. But, whether you're an all-out, multicolor illustrator or a simple, black-and-white journal-keeper, the key is to get started now. Claim your Bible; personalize it; celebrate your style; and do whatever it takes to transform your Bible from a casual acquaintance into a BFF. Today.

Your Personal Top 5: Starting Out

Try to think of five specific things you can do, or five specific supplies you need, to begin illustrating your faith. Write them down in the space below.

1. _____

2. _____

3. _____

4. _____

5. _____

Those who listen to instruction will prosper; those who trust the LORD will be joyful.

PROVERBS 16:20 NLT

Your Personal Top 10:
What Is God Trying to Say?

On the lines below, make a list of ten specific messages that you think God may be trying to tell you. If you have trouble coming up with ten, try opening your Bible to a few of your favorite passages and see what happens.

1. _____

2. _____

3. _____

4. _____

5. _____

6. _____

7. _____

8. _____

9. _____

10. _____

Let us hold fast the confession of our hope without wavering, for He who promised is faithful.
HEBREWS 10:23 NASB

Great is Thy faithfulness.
LAMENTATIONS 3:23 KJV

God is faithful; you were called into fellowship with His Son, Jesus Christ our Lord.
I CORINTHIANS 1:9 HCSB

I will sing about the LORD's faithful love forever; I will proclaim Your faithfulness to all generations with my mouth.
PSALM 89:1 HCSB

#4

Write Love Letters to God

"This vast ocean of love cannot be measured or explained, but it can be experienced."

SARAH YOUNG

My husband and I started dating in high school. That's when we began exchanging love letters. Thankfully, we've kept all those letters, and we still reread them from time to time. When we find a quiet moment at the end of the day, or when we're home alone and in a sentimental mood, we pull out the box that contains those old familiar letters, and we begin reading them to each other. It's a magical experience that reminds us of how much we've grown as individuals and, more importantly, as a couple.

Our high school love letters were, not surprisingly, somewhat naïve. But those love letters were—and still are—meaningful because they recorded the honest emotions that Jonathan and I felt as we began our journey. Now, after seventeen years of marriage, we can look back with the benefit of time and the perspective of adulthood. We understand that the letters are, in some ways, juvenile; in other ways, profound. But every single one is a treasure, a precious little gift from the past that grows more beautiful with each passing year.

If you paid attention to the title of this chapter, you already know where I'm going with this. So, I'll give you the benefit of the doubt and assume that you've figured out the point I'm trying to make: this chapter is about expressing your love *for* God *to* God. In writing.

Why? Several reasons.

First and foremost, we should express our love for God because the Word teaches us to do so. We're instructed to praise Him and thank Him and honor Him and love Him. This is what Jesus was talking about when He put forth the greatest commandment: to love the Lord with all our hearts. Although Jesus didn't say anything specifically about *writing* love letters to God, I think He'd certainly approve.

And there's another good reason to express your love for God in writing: when you take pen to paper, you create a written record of your experiences, a personal history in black and white of your unfolding relationship with the Lord. If you express your emotions honestly and often, you'll soon have a boxful of letters, each one revealing a different aspect of your faith journey. These love letters you write to God are, quite literally, gifts you give to Him *and* to yourself.

For God so loved the world, that He gave His only begotten Son, that whosoever believeth in Him should not perish, but have everlasting life.

JOHN 3:16 KJV

Spiritual Maturity: It Happens

"A Christian is never in a state of completion but always in the process of becoming."
MARTIN LUTHER

God doesn't intend that we stand still in our faith. He wants us to keep growing. When we fall in love with our Bibles and with the Author who wrote them, we grow as individuals *and* as Christians. The growth may be imperceptible at first, but before long, we begin to see our world and our lives differently. Our priorities begin to change, our attitudes begin to change, and our behaviors begin to change as we gain insights and maturity.

No matter our age, no matter our responsibilities, no matter our circumstances, we all have opportunities to learn, to serve, and to grow. Wherever we happen to be, God is there too, and He wants to bless us with an expanding array of spiritual gifts. Our job is to let Him.

The path to spiritual maturity unfolds one day at a time. In the quiet moments when we open our hearts to the Lord, the Creator who made us keeps remaking us. He gives us wisdom, perspective, patience, and strength. Speaking of strength, all of us need it from time to time because life's path isn't always smooth. Many of life's most important lessons are painful to learn. During tough times, God stands ready to protect us. As Psalm 147:3 promises, "He heals the brokenhearted and bandages their wounds" (NCV). In His own good time, God always heals our hearts if we open them to Him.

But spiritual growth doesn't only take place when times are tough. Every day of life—whether good, bad, or in between—offers the opportunity to grow closer to the Creator as we walk and talk with Him. God is always available, always ready to lead, to love, and to teach. When we're ready to talk about our feelings (or write about them), He's ready to listen. The more we talk, and the more we write, the more we grow.

\# \# \# \# \# \# \# \# \#

"Grow, dear friends,
but grow,
I beseech you,
in God's way, which is
the only true way."

HANNAH WHITALL SMITH

\# \# \# \# \# \# \# \# \#

The Letters Go Both Ways

"The Bible is God's love letter to us."
BILLY GRAHAM

The Bible is filled with passages that express, either directly or indirectly, God's love for us. He created us. He's intimately involved in our lives. He promises to protect us now and forever. And His Son demonstrated total love for us on the cross. These are not trivial matters. These expressions of God's love are foundational to the Christian experience. These promises can, and should, comprise the cornerstone upon which we build our lives.

As Billy Graham observed, the Bible is God's message of love to mankind. But you needn't think of it as a love letter to all humanity; you can think of it as a personal correspondence addressed specifically to you. In truth, your love letters to God are direct responses to His love letter to you.

God's love for you is deeper, wider, higher, and grander than you can imagine. He knows you better than you know yourself,

He has a plan for your life, and His compassion is infinite. He expresses Himself in many ways, some of which

"The Bible is a letter from God with our personal address on it."

SØREN KIERKEGAARD

are understated or subtle. But the Bible is not one of God's subtle communications. It is a black-and-white expression of His love for mankind—and for you.

Today and every day, as you carve out a few quiet moments for thanksgiving and praise, remember that the Lord is always with you. He is not just near; He is here. And He's already written His love letter to you.

Now, He's waiting patiently for your response.

✗✗ ✗ ✗ ✗ ✗ ✗ ✗ ✗ ✗

"Nothing can separate you from God's love, absolutely nothing. God is enough for time, God is enough for eternity. God is enough!"

HANNAH WHITALL SMITH

"A bird
does not know
it can fly before
it uses its wings.
We learn God's love
in our hearts
as soon as
we act upon it."

CORRIE TEN BOOM

See How You've Changed

*"It matters little where a person
may be at this moment;
the point is whether he is growing."*
GEORGE MACDONALD

One of the major benefits of writing messages to God is that you get to keep them! That means you can reread them whenever you like. And as you continue to grow in your faith, you can look back on the earlier stages of your spiritual journey to see how you've progressed. And make no mistake: you *are* going to progress. The act of writing down your thoughts and addressing them to God can be a transformational experience.

Your world keeps changing, and so do you. The question is not *if* you will change but *how* will you change. Your written correspondence to the Creator will provide a permanent narrative of the changes you experience on your spiritual journey.

Even if you've never kept a journal before—even if you don't like your handwriting *or* your writing style—I strongly suggest that you give it a try: write a few letters to God and see how it works for you. If you become a regular letter writer, I predict that those

"Becoming like Christ is a long, slow process of growth."

RICK WARREN

notes will become treasured keepsakes, like the letters that Jonathan and I exchanged in high school. Just as our letters are a blessing to us, your letters to the Lord will be a blessing to you. So don't delay. It's never too early, or too late, to begin expressing yourself to God *in writing*.

"Love Him totally who gave Himself totally for your love."

CLARE OF ASSISI

"We set our eyes on the finish line, forgetting the past, and straining toward the mark of spiritual maturity and fruitfulness."

VONETTE BRIGHT

Your Personal Top 5: Things You Need to Say

Try to think of five things you *really* need to say to God. Jot them down in the space below.

1. _____

2. _____

3. _____

4. _____

5. _____

P.S. Where in the Bible can we seek Him in these thoughts?

This is love for God: to obey His commands.

I JOHN 5:3 NIV

Your Personal Top 10:
Gifts You're Thankful For

On the lines below, make a list of ten things that you're thankful for. By the way, these blessings can be topics for future love letters and thank-you notes to the Giver of all these gifts.

1. _____

2. _____

3. _____

4. _____

5. _____

6. _____

7. _____

8. _____

9. _____

10. _____

*He said to him, "You shall love the Lord your God
with all your heart, with all your soul,
and with all your mind. This is the greatest
and most important command."*
MATTHEW 22:37-38 HCSB

*I love the LORD, for He heard my voice;
He heard my cry for mercy.*
PSALM 116:1 NIV

We love Him, because He first loved us.
I JOHN 4:19 KJV

*We know that all things work together
for the good of those who love God:
those who are called according to His purpose.*
ROMANS 8:28 HCSB

#5

Get Your Daily Dose

"I believe the reason so many are failing today is that they have not disciplined themselves to read God's Word consistently, day in and day out, and to apply it to every situation in life."

KAY ARTHUR

You and I both know that the world has a way of filling up every square inch of our calendar space with things to do, places to go, people to see, and responsibilities to fulfill. Add to the mix the tsunami of modern media—social and otherwise—and you've got a very long to-do list. So do your friends. And so do I. But I think I can speak for all of us when I say that no matter how busy we are, no matter how many obligations we have or how many people we must care for, we still have time for God *if*, that is, we *make* time for Him.

And shouldn't we make time for Him? Really? After all, we find the time to do so many less important things. So shouldn't we be able to squeeze in a few minutes of Jesus time every day? Of course we should. But sometimes we convince ourselves that we're simply too busy, or that there aren't enough hours in the day to get everything done. So we hurry and scurry from place to place, trying to tick things off our to-do lists while leaving some very important things undone. Then, when the day draws to a close and we switch off the lights, what's left undone? Spending time with God, that's what's left undone.

Been there. Done that. Maybe you have too.

Of course, the problem with the "not enough hours in the day" argument is that it's simply untrue. There's always time for God if we make Him a priority, but there's never enough time for Him if we don't.

The fallacy with the "too busy" proposition is that it, too, is untrue. After all, we manage to find time for a wide range of diversions, distractions, pastimes, and amusements. Most of us watch TV every day. We go online every day; we check e-mail, snail mail, and text messages every day. Truth be told, many of us are so consumed by twenty-first-century time gobblers that we invest several hours each day simply looking at screens or talking into smartphones. We can find time for these tasks but can't figure out a way to spend a couple of quiet minutes with the Creator. Ouch! The truth hurts!

"Don't fall into the trap of being constantly on the go."

SARAH YOUNG

We live in a society that seems to glorify busyness.

✝ ✝ ✝ ✝ ✝ ✝ ✝ ✝ ✝

"Whatever God is urging you to clear away cannot begin to be compared to what He ultimately wants to bring you."

BETH MOORE

✝ ✝ ✝ ✝ ✝ ✝ ✝ ✝ ✝

Being overcommitted has attained a certain glamour factor: it makes us feel important. So we load up our calendars, tap our screens, and go, go, go. But in truth, our time belongs first to Jesus.

Here's my point in a nutshell: if you want to fall in love with your Bible, you've got to fall in love with it *every day*.

Not every other day.

Not on weekends.

Not once in a while.

Not when Old Man Trouble rings the doorbell.

Every day.

Until it becomes a habit.

Period.

"If you do the same thing every day at the same time for the same length of time, you'll save yourself from many a problem. Routine is a condition of survival."

FLANNERY O'CONNER

Make It a Habit

"Your little choices become habits that affect
the bigger decisions you make in life."
ELIZABETH GEORGE

It's an old saying and a true one: "First, you make your habits, and then your habits make you." No habit is more important to your spiritual health than the habit of getting in touch with God every day. When it comes to your relationship with Him, consistency is key. To experience the full measure of God's blessings, you need to make your time with Him so natural, so tightly woven into the fabric of your day, that you don't even need to put it on your to-do list. Once it's a firmly established habit, spending time with your Creator won't be something that you write down and check off; it will be something that happens every day, as a matter of course.

Some people say it takes two weeks to establish a habit. Others say it takes twenty-one days, or a month, maybe two. I suppose it depends on both the person and the habit. But when it comes to reading your Bible every day, I think you and I can safely agree that the first month is the hardest. When you've picked up that book for thirty days straight, day thirty-one doesn't seem so hard. Here's my suggestion: try it for a month. Do whatever it takes to spend time in God's Word every single day for just thirty days, and see if it becomes a habit. I predict that it will.

Have It Your Way

*"You don't have to look like everybody else
to be acceptable and accepted."*
FRED ROGERS

It takes time to establish a regular routine that includes God, but there's no law that says you've got to read your Bible first thing in the morning. If your best time is in the evening, feel free. Or maybe lunchtime is your best time to focus on the Word. Again, it's your choice. Whatever works.

This is the day the Lord has made; let us rejoice and be glad in it.

PSALM 118:24 HCSB

I like to diversify my readings and split them up into little bites throughout the day. In fact, I try to have a running conversation with God all day long. Then, in the evening, I take time to reflect on the day and make journal entries.

As you can probably tell, I like variety. In fact, the thought of doing the same thing every day seems a little scary to me. But what works for me may not work for you, and that's perfectly okay. You may be more comfortable with a set schedule. If so, maybe you'll want to tackle one of those read-the-Bible-in-a-year plans. Again, the best strategy is the one that fits your personality, your learning style, and your timetable.

"Sow an act and you reap a habit; sow a habit and you reap a character; sow a character and you reap a destiny."

FRANCES E. WILLARD

I find that my time with God works best when I plan ahead, so on Sunday, I jot down devotion topics for the coming week. On Monday, I may focus on sermon notes; or, on Tuesday, I may explore a passage from a book I'm reading. Wednesday, Thursday, Friday, and Saturday have their own topics too. For me, this strategy works well because it gives me ready-to-use ideas to jump-start my conversations with God. And I've found that the more often I talk to Him, the more intimate our conversations become.

Morning by morning
He wakens me and opens
my understanding to His will.
The Sovereign LORD
has spoken to me,
and I have listened.

ISAIAH 50:4-5 NLT

When You Talk to Him Every Day, the Conversation Changes

"The manifold rewards of a serious,
consistent prayer life demonstrate clearly
that time with our Lord should be our first priority."
SHIRLEY DOBSON

When you talk to someone almost every day, the conversation usually flows. You can pick right up where you left off yesterday, with no need for explanations, no need for clarifications, and no need for formality. It's different if you're meeting somebody for the first time, or if you're trying to reconnect with someone you haven't talked to in a while. Those conversations often become surface-level exchanges. They're less intimate, less impactful, more reserved.

And it works the same way with God.

When you talk to Him every day—and when you listen carefully to the messages He places on your heart—it's almost like talking to your best friend. There's a comfort level borne of familiarity. You don't have to explain things or re-explain them. You don't wonder if you're getting your point across. You know that you can share your true feelings without the need to sugarcoat them. You can tell Him anything and everything. But just as importantly, you can listen, carefully and quietly. When you do, the monologue ends and a true dialogue begins.

Thus begins one of the most beautiful experiences in the Christian faith: a two-way conversation with God.

Listen Carefully

"The purpose of all prayer is to find God's will and to make that our prayer."

CATHERINE MARSHALL

It's easy to talk to God. Just close your eyes and start praying. In fact, you don't even have to close your eyes; He hears open-eyed prayers too! You say a prayer; He hears it, every time without fail. The human-to-God line of communication is always open.

But not so in the other direction.

Sometimes when God speaks to us, we're too busy or too distracted to notice. Instead of quieting ourselves long enough to hear His voice or sense His guidance, we succumb to the noise around us, or to the self-generated noise within us.

Occasionally, God speaks loudly and clearly. Think stone tablets, burning bushes, or Saul on the road to Damascus. But usually, our Father speaks in a quieter voice: He doesn't shout; He whispers. And if we're wise, we'll be listening carefully.

Are you willing to pray and to listen carefully (and quietly) for God's response? Hopefully so. Don't expect stone tablets or burning bushes. More often, He communicates in subtler ways. So if you really want to hear His voice, you'll have to be a good listener.

"Deep within the center of the soul is a chamber of peace where God lives and where, if we will enter it and quiet all the other sounds, we can hear His gentle whisper."

LETTIE COWMAN

"Prayer begins
by talking to God,
but it ends by
listening to Him.
In the face of
Absolute Truth,
silence is the
soul's language."

BISHOP FULTON J. SHEEN

Don't Let the World Cheat You Out of Your Daily Dose

Because our world is filled with temptations and distractions, you and I confront them at every turn. We're constantly being tempted to address the world's priorities first and God's priorities later. But when we relegate God to the back corners of our lives—or ignore Him altogether—we do ourselves and our loved ones a great disservice.

We live in the world, but we must not worship it. Our duty is to place God first and everything else second.

Your world, like mine, is a busy, noisy, distraction-filled place. The world seems to cry, "Worship me with your time, your money, your energy, and your thoughts!" But God has a better plan: He wants us to worship Him and Him alone; everything else must be secondary.

Don't let the world rob you of the joy and abundance that inevitably results when you spend time with the Lord every day. He deserves your praise. And you deserve the experience of giving it to Him.

"An ongoing relationship with God through His Word is essential to the Christian's consistent victory."

BETH MOORE

Your Personal Top 5: Devo Topics

List five topics that you'd like to explore in your upcoming daily devos. Write them in the space below.

1. _____

2. _____

3. _____

4. _____

5. _____

"Energy and time are limited entities. Therefore, we need to use them wisely, focusing on what is truly important."

SARAH YOUNG

Your Personal Top 10: Distractions

On the lines below, make a list of ten distractions that keep you from focusing on more important stuff (like the spiritual stuff).

1. _____

2. _____

3. _____

4. _____

5. _____

6. _____

7. _____

8. _____

9. _____

10. _____

*Morning by morning He wakens me and opens
my understanding to His will. The Sovereign LORD
has spoken to me, and I have listened.*

ISAIAH 50:4-5 NLT

*It is good to give thanks to the LORD,
And to sing praises to Your name, O Most High.*

PSALM 92:1 NKJV

*All scripture is given by inspiration of God,
and is profitable for doctrine, for reproof,
for correction, for instruction in righteousness.*

II TIMOTHY 3:16 KJV

*But grow in the grace and knowledge of
our Lord and Savior Jesus Christ. To Him be the glory
both now and to the day of eternity. Amen.*

II PETER 3:18 HCSB

#6

Be a Fangirl

"Become so wrapped up in something that you forget to be afraid."

LADY BIRD JOHNSON

Maybe you don't see yourself as a fangirl, but I'll bet you were once. Once upon a time, I'll bet you were head over heels for some teenage heartthrob, or some boy band, or some good-looking movie star. C'mon, admit it. Long ago and far away, you actually had a monumental crush on some unattainable object of your affections. And you considered yourself the world's biggest fan.

If we are being honest about our preteen fangirl moments, I just have to give a shout-out to New Kids on the Block! Yes, I know I might be dating myself here, but I'll never forget my tenth birthday—the year was 1990— which was floor-to-ceiling NKOTB. Somehow, my mom managed to find NKOTB tablecloths, cups, banners, the whole nine yards.

I, of course, came out in a white jumpsuit, two layers of scrunchie socks (aqua and purple), with my hair up in two layers of scrunchies (of course, aqua and purple to match my socks), and a three-inch New Kids on the Block button proudly displayed on my white jumpsuit.

Folks, this was obviously the top of my style game. It was a magical moment in time: a room full of screeching fangirls singing karaoke and writing love letters to Jordan Knight! This is what fangirl moments are made of!

Do you remember how exciting it felt to be totally captivated and enthralled? Do you remember what it felt like to be a super fan? Do you recall how happy it made you feel to think about—and talk about—the object of your fandom? Well, as Christians, we should feel *even more* enthusiasm for Jesus. We should be excited about our faith. *Really* excited. But all too often, we're not.

For teenage girls, it's socially acceptable to be "fan-ish," but for those of us who are grown women, not so much. As we leave the teenage years behind, most of us begin to take life a little more seriously. We're expected to become mature women, and we experience unspoken societal pressures to grow up. So we take down the boy-band posters. We give the fangirl memorabilia to Goodwill. And we pass on to adulthood. No more swoons or squeals. Like it or not, that's life.

I guess it's like the man says in Ecclesiastes: there's a time for everything:

A time to reap, a time to sow.
A time to laugh, a time to cry.
A time to be a teenage fangirl, and a time to grow up.
(I made the last one up, but I happen to think it's true.)

It's perfectly natural, even healthy, to graduate from those teen or tween fandom crushes. But when it comes to our relationship with Jesus, we should never outgrow the fangirl mindset. We should never allow ourselves to become too mature to express our enthusiasm for Jesus. We should be fangirls for Christ, and never outgrow those feelings.

"We act as though comfort and luxury were the chief requirements of life, when all we need to make us really happy is something to be enthusiastic about."

CHARLES KINGSLEY

Enthusiasm Is Contagious

"Be enthusiastic.
Every occasion is an opportunity to do good."
RUSSELL CONWELL

Enthusiastic Christianity is contagious. If you enjoy a life-altering relationship with Jesus, that relationship will have an impact on others—perhaps a profound impact.

As a Christian, you have so many reasons to be enthusiastic about your life, your faith, your opportunities, and your future. Do you need me to remind you about some of the big blessings? Well, first and foremost, God loves you, and as an expression of that love, He sent His Son so that you might have eternal life. Plus, God has given you a guidebook for life: the Bible.

Need more things to get excited about? Consider the fact that God has sent you friends and family to share and enrich your life. And consider the fact that each new day is an opportunity to serve Him and spread the good news.

Still not convinced? Then grab some paper and start making a *detailed* list of your blessings. Don't just focus on the big stuff. Also take

"It is not enough to reach for the brass ring. You must also enjoy the merry-go-round."

JULIE ANDREWS

notice of the everyday blessings that you're tempted to take for granted. When you begin noticing the smaller blessings, things like chirping birds and smiling babies, you'll quickly realize that it's impossible to notice them all, much less write them all down. But one thing's for sure: the more time you spend counting your blessings, the more gratitude you'll feel in your heart. And the more excited you'll become.

"Instead of living a black-and-white existence, we'll be released into a Technicolor world of vibrancy and emotion when we more accurately reflect His nature to the world around us."

BILL HYBELS

(Too) Safe on the Sidelines?

"When your heart is ablaze with the love of God,
then you love other people—especially the rip-snorting
sinners—so much that you dare to tell them
about Jesus with no apologies and no fear."
CATHERINE MARSHALL

Perhaps you're thinking, "It's easy for you, Shanna, to be a highly vocal Bible fan. You're a pastor's wife. And you've got Illustrated Faith. But I'm not very comfortable talking about my faith. To me, it seems a little over-the-top."

If that's what you're thinking, I'll let you in on a little secret: I'm an introvert too. At our house, Jonathan is the extrovert, not me. So I think I understand some of the reservations you may feel when it comes to sharing your faith. Maybe you're just plain shy. Or maybe you're concerned that other people may judge you. Perhaps you're afraid because you don't think you know enough about the Bible, or because you haven't had a dramatic Damascus-Road conversion story to share. Actually, there are hundreds of possible reasons that talking about Jesus may be difficult for you, but they all boil down to one single fact: for whatever reason, you just feel safer keeping your faith—and your excitement—to yourself.

My suggestion is don't overthink it and don't box yourself in.

Here in the twenty-first century, you don't have to have a super sales personality with a scales-falling-off-the-eyes conversion experience to be an effective, expressive fan of Jesus. Why? Because social media allows you to interact with people without the added pressure of face-to-face encounters.

So I've got a couple of suggestions. Actually, they're experiments.

Experiment #1: Try a face-to-face expression of your excitement for Christ with another human being. Just one. To see if it's actually as painful as you imagine it to be. Ask God to lead you to a person who needs to hear about His Son. I'm not asking you to change the world or turn water into wine. I'm just asking you to look for a single soul who needs to hear the good news *in person* from an excited Christian. When the Lord leads you to that person (notice I said *when*, not *if*), just share what Jesus has meant to you. This little experiment may be a bit daunting, but it has the potential for big rewards. So try to have an honest conversation—in person—with just one living, breathing human being. One testimony. A single trial run. To see how it feels.

Experiment #2: Express your fandom in social media. Actually, this is my preferred style of communication. Whether it's Facebook, Instagram, Pinterest, Periscope, or any of the other platforms, I like the introvert-friendly

> "Wherever you are, be all there. Live to the hilt every situation you believe to be the will of God."
>
> JIM ELLIOT

nature of Internet communications. Digital interactions make it easier for me to express myself. And when you begin expressing your fandom for God online, I promise you'll find an unlimited supply of people who can benefit from your enthusiasm and your encouragement. When you do, it will set you apart from the great mass of passive Christians who've never shared their faith with *anybody.*

Far too many Christians are too reserved, too timid, too fearful, or too busy to discuss their relationship to the Creator. I'm not picking on these people because I'm sure they've got their reasons for staying safely on the sidelines. I had my reasons too when I was a sideline-sitter. And as an introvert, I know how hard it can be to express emotions. But there's an ironic twist to this picture. Many of these people, the same ones who checked the box marked "Christian" on the census form, are *very* excited about other things; they're just not excited about their faith.

So what *are* they excited about? The answer is . . . [you fill in the blank].

The blank, of course, can be just about anything: money, media, sports, politics, fashion, food, gossip, or a thousand other things. In truth, these excited aficionados are simply grownup fangirls or fanguys, only they've traded in one worldly obsession for another.

By the way, talking about worldly preoccupations is often easier than talking about God. But as Christians, we're instructed to share the good news, and that's exactly what we should do, even if sharing it involves a little personal risk.

When we consider the personal sacrifice that Jesus made for us, shouldn't we be excited to tell His story? And shouldn't we be fans? The answer is obvious.

For God has not given us a spirit of fear and timidity, but of power, love, and self-discipline. So never be ashamed to tell others about our Lord.

II TIMOTHY 1:7-8 NLT

"If we are
going to experience
joy in this lifetime,
there's only one possible way:
We have to choose it.
We will to choose it in
the middle of a situation
that seems too hard to bear.
We have to choose it
even if our worst nightmare
comes true."

KAY WARREN

Take the Risk: Get Excited

"Each day, look for a kernel of excitement."
BARBARA JORDAN

Standing up for your beliefs, whether face-to-face or online, always involves some risk. But if you're standing up for the *right* beliefs, it's worth it.

So what are the risks? Well, some people may think you're over-the-top. Others may think you're being a little too pushy. Still others, the folks who are totally uninterested, may ignore you altogether. But once in a while (actually, more often than you might think), you'll make a connection with someone who needs to hear the message *from you*. At that moment, you're no longer just a *fan*, you're also God's *ambassador*, which, by the way, is one of the most important jobs on earth.

When you stop to think about it, you'll have to admit that this world already has an ample supply of lukewarm Christians. If you don't believe me, just Google "church attendance statistics." But the world is in desperate need of *excited* Christians who are willing to stand up for their faith.

As you think about the gifts God has given you, do you feel a little bit of that fangirl-type enthusiasm returning? Can you feel the passion? Can you harness the enthusiasm? I hope so. And I hope you'll share your excitement with a world that needs more women (like you) who are absolutely thrilled to be fans of the Father and the Son.

Your Personal Top 5:
When You're Silent (But Shouldn't Be)

Think about the way you express your faith. Then try to think of five ways that you've been holding back. In other words, try to think of examples when you might have expressed your love for Jesus but didn't. Then jot them down in the space below.

1. _____

2. _____

3. _____

4. _____

5. _____

I will thank Yahweh with all my heart;
I will declare all Your wonderful works.
I will rejoice and boast about You;
I will sing about Your name, Most High.

PSALM 9:1-2 HCSB

Your Personal Top 10: Personal Experiences

On the lines below, make a list of ten personal experiences that have impacted your faith journey. Then consider how you might share these experiences with others.

1. _____

2. _____

3. _____

4. _____

5. _____

6. _____

7. _____

8. _____

9. _____

10. _____

All those who stand before others and say
they believe in Me, I will say before my Father
in heaven that they belong to Me.
MATTHEW 10:32 NCV

And I say to you, anyone who acknowledges
Me before men, the Son of Man will
also acknowledge him before the angels of God.
LUKE 12:8 HCSB

Then He said to them, "Go into all the world
and preach the gospel to the whole creation."
MARK 16:15 HCSB

Whatever you do, do it enthusiastically,
as something done for the Lord and not for men.
COLOSSIANS 3:23 HCSB

#7

Apply the Lessons

"There's some task which the God of all the universe, the great Creator, has for you to do, and which will remain undone and incomplete, until by faith and obedience, you step into the will of God."

ALAN REDPATH

Reading the Bible is part comprehension and part application, with strong emphasis on the latter. Now it's time to talk about the application part. I think you know what I'm talking about. It's all about turning biblical principles into practical applications of your faith.

The more you read your Bible, the more lessons you'll learn. And the more lessons you learn, the more you'll want to apply those lessons to the situations you encounter in everyday life. After all, the reason you learned all those lessons in the first place was to use them. And the teachings we find in God's Word remain theoretical constructs until we find ways to turn them into reality.

Two thousand years ago, James, the brother of Jesus, made it clear that it's never enough to hear God's words or to read them. We must also act upon them.

But don't just listen to God's word. You must do what it says. Otherwise, you are only fooling yourselves. For if you listen to the word and don't obey, it is like glancing at your face in a mirror. You see yourself, walk away, and forget what you look like. But if you look carefully into the perfect law that sets you free, and if you do what it says and don't forget what you heard, then God will bless you for doing it.
JAMES 1:22–25 NLT

But James doesn't stop there. He took it up another notch in chapter 2.

What good is it, dear brothers and sisters, if you say you have faith but don't show it by your actions? Can that kind of faith save anyone? Suppose you see a brother or sister who has no food or clothing, and you say, "Good-bye and have a good day; stay warm and eat well"—but then you don't give that person any food or clothing. What good does that do? So you see, faith by itself isn't enough. Unless it produces good deeds, it is dead and useless.
JAMES 2:14–17 NLT

Ouch! That's tough talk. But there it is, in black and white, right there in the New Testament. So, when James says that faith without works is dead, we have no choice but to believe him. And then we must get busy turning our faith into deeds.

Jesus told the story of the Good Samaritan, a man who helped a fellow traveler when no one else would. We, too, should be Good Samaritans when we find

"Doing something positive toward another person is a practical approach to feeling good about yourself."

BARBARA JOHNSON

people who need a helping hand or a pat on the back. Those people, by the way, are all around us. When we look for them, we will find them. Helping them is never a burden. Instead, it's an opportunity to express our faith in a tangible way.

Zora Neale Hurston noted, "When you find a man who has lost his way, you don't make fun of him and scorn him and leave him there. You show him the way. If you don't do that, you just prove that you're sort of lost yourself."

The implication is clear: when you find your faith, you'll soon find a way to express it, in words *and* in deeds.

"Your wealth of experience makes you rich. Spend it on hurt people. They need it so badly."

BETH MOORE

Positive Changes

*"God's ultimate goal for your life
on earth is not comfort,
but character development. He wants you
to grow up spiritually and become like Christ."*

RICK WARREN

God gave us the Word for a very good reason: to use it. When we do—when we integrate biblical principles into the fabric of our lives—we begin to experience real, positive changes. Sometimes these changes are relatively easy; sometimes they're not. But we can be certain that whenever we apply God's lessons to challenges of everyday living, we'll be better off in the long run.

You and I are always changing. Life moves on and so do we. The challenge, of course, is to change in *positive* ways. We want to get better (like a fine wine), not bitter (like a fine whine). So how can we do it? Regular Bible reading is a great place to start.

It's impossible to read your Bible seriously every day and not be changed by the experience.

"The measure of a life, after all, is not its duration but its donation."

CORRIE TEN BOOM

The act of picking up God's Word day after day will, in time, transform the way you see the world and react to it. The stronger your relationship with Jesus, the more you'll want to be like Him. And you'll want to follow Him, even when it's hard.

And make no mistake: sometimes it's *very* hard.

"He that is mastered by Christ is the master of every circumstance. Does the circumstance press hard against you? Do not push it away. It is the Potter's hand."

LETTIE COWMAN

Strength for the Struggles

"Every difficult task that comes across your path—
every one that you would rather not do,
that will take the most effort, cause the most pain,
and be the greatest struggle—brings a blessing with it."
LETTIE COWMAN

Face facts: sometimes, life is just plain tough. Bad things happen, and we don't always understand why, but we're forced to move on with our lives anyway, whether we're ready or not. It's no wonder, then, that even the most inspired Christian women can, from time to time, find themselves running on empty.

When we find ourselves tired, discouraged, or worse, there's a source from which we can draw the energy needed to recharge our spiritual batteries. That source is God. When we turn everything over to Him day by day, He has a way of restoring our strength and healing our hearts *eventually*. Our job is to wait patiently—and listen attentively—until He does.

"God will make obstacles serve His purpose."
LETTIE COWMAN

Andrew Murray observed, "Where there is much prayer, there will be much of the Spirit; where there is much of the Spirit, there will be ever-increasing power." These words remind us that the ultimate source of our strength is the Lord. When we turn to Him for solace, we will not be disappointed.

"Often God has to shut a door in our face so that He can subsequently open the door through which He wants us to go."

CATHERINE MARSHALL

By falling in love with your Bible, you are, in a very real way, insuring yourself against "the slings and arrows of outrageous fortune" (I don't usually quote Shakespeare, but this time I decided to make an exception). God's Word serves as a defense against the world's demands, a buffer against the heartaches and disappointments that befall us all.

Recently, I experienced a personal struggle that turned out differently than I first expected. And I know if I hadn't been seeking Him in the Word, things would have turned out badly.

My husband and I were deep in prayer and conversation over something that frustrated us both. So we handed it over to God and asked for His guidance. As sometimes happens (okay, *often* happens), God gave us an answer that we *didn't* want. Had we not been grounded in His Word and guidance, we could have easily justified going in the opposite direction. But our deepest desire is to follow Him. And that's precisely what we did.

Knowing that we can trust the Lord in those times when our hearts are torn brings us so much peace, and it makes it so much easier to follow His guidance (even though we may *think* we want something else). After handing our lives over to Him and going to Him for those big decisions, it is now so much easier to look back and see how He is *always* there, in the small moments and large. So as Jonathan and I handed over this frustration to Him, we had a sense of peace and understanding knowing that we were doing the right thing because we were following our Father.

The next time you're facing one of life's inevitable struggles, slow yourself down long enough to have a quiet chat—or a series of chats—with your Father in heaven. When you do, you'll discover that the Creator of the universe has the power to make all things new. . . including you.

‡ ‡ ‡ ‡ ‡ ‡ ‡ ‡ ‡

"When a train goes through a tunnel and it gets dark, you don't throw away your ticket and jump off.
You sit still and trust the engineer."

CORRIE TEN BOOM

Be Quick to Be Kind

"To show great love for God and our neighbor,
we need not do great things.
It is how much love we put in the doing
that makes our offering something beautiful for God."
MOTHER TERESA

In your dealings with other people, always try to check things out with God. Test things out through prayer and Scripture reading. And don't ever be afraid to surprise other people with unexpected kindnesses. Our friends and neighbors need all the encouragement they can get, and we need the experience of encouraging them.

Since we're never promised tomorrow, today is the best day to be compassionate.

St. Teresa of Avila observed, "There are only two duties required of us—the love of God and the love of our neighbor, and the surest sign of discovering whether we observe these duties is the love of our neighbor." Her words remind us that we honor God by serving our friends and neighbors with kind words, heartfelt prayers, and helping hands.

"Authentic faith cannot help but act."

BETH MOORE

God instructs us to share our blessings with the world. He wants us to act on His behalf as we look for opportunities to spread kindness wherever we go. When we do, everybody wins.

"You can always give without loving, but you can never love without giving."

AMY CARMICHAEL

Your Personal Top 5: Ways to Apply Your Faith

Try to think of five practical ways you can apply your faith within the next twenty-four hours. Write them down in the space below.

1. _____

2. _____

3. _____

4. _____

5. _____

"As faithful stewards of what we have, ought we not to give earnest thought to our staggering surplus?"

ELISABETH ELLIOT

Your Personal Top 10: People Who Need Your Encouragement or Help

On the lines below, make a list of ten people who need a pat on the back, a helping hand, or both. Hint: these people represent ways that you can apply your faith very soon.

1. _____

2. _____

3. _____

4. _____

5. _____

6. _____

7. _____

8. _____

9. _____

10. _____

Carry one another's burdens;
in this way you will fulfill the law of Christ.
GALATIANS 6:2 HCSB

Prove yourselves doers of the word,
and not merely hearers who delude themselves.
JAMES 1:22 NASB

For truly I say to you,
if you have faith the size of a mustard seed,
you will say to this mountain,
"Move from here to there,"
and it will move;
and nothing will be impossible to you.
MATTHEW 17:20 NASB

Whatever you did for one of the least
of these brothers of Mine, you did for Me.
MATTHEW 25:40 HCSB

#8

Bible, Coffee, and Girlfriends

"Friends are like a quilt with lots of different shapes, sizes, colors, and patterns of fabric. But the end result brings you warmth and comfort in a support system that makes your life richer and fuller."

SUZANNE DALE EZELL

I really don't think God intends for any of us to be solitary Christians. That's why He brings friends into our lives. He wants us to talk things over and help each other out. He wants us to be strong together. He wants us to bless our friends and vice versa.

My girlfriends enrich my life in so many ways: they teach me things. They offer me encouragement. They make me think. They make me laugh. When they think I'm wrong, they tell me so. When they think I'm right, they tell me that too. When I'm down, they lift me up, and when I'm up, they help me celebrate. My friends have contributed so much to my life and my faith that I'm informally dedicating this chapter to them. (Okay,

"*We are all travelers in the desert of life and the best we can find in our journey is an honest friend.*"

ROBERT LOUIS STEVENSON

girls, you know who you are.)

But you might be wondering what all this friendship talk has to do with the main topic of this book. The answer is actually pretty simple: my friends also help me stay fired up about my faith. And I try to keep them fired up too. Oftentimes, we do it over coffee.

Put me at a corner table in a nice coffee shop, give me my journaling Bible, add a few of my best girlfriends, and I'm a very happy camper. When we start talking about God's Word and God's works, the real joy begins. By sharing personal experiences, we strengthen each other. Sometimes, our discussions are total encouragement from beginning to end. But when we need to challenge each other, we do. And that's good, because sometimes it's by challenging each other that we make each other stronger.

"Cherish your human connections: your relationships with friends and family."

BARBARA BUSH

True Friends Challenge Us

"A friend is one who makes me do my best."
OSWALD CHAMBERS

None of us are perfect. We all have lessons to learn, we all have issues to work through, and we all come up with wrongheaded ideas from time to time. That's why we need friends who are honest enough—and strong enough—to speak up when they think we're heading in the wrong direction. These friends, the ones who aren't afraid to speak their minds, are invaluable resources. By challenging us, they make us stronger.

"A faithful friend is a strong defense."

LOUISA MAY ALCOTT

Offering a contrary opinion can be hard sometimes; listening to a contrary opinion can be even harder. But honest dialogue helps us grow. And constructive criticism, when offered with compassion and love, may be just what we need to make positive changes or mid-course corrections.

When you're talking to friends, don't be afraid to speak your mind, and don't be afraid to ask the tough questions. You can be sure that your friend needs honesty more than flattery.

And the same goes for you: if a friend offers you constructive criticism—or challenges you in some other way—listen. It may be sound advice, whether you like it or not.

The world is filled with yes-men and yes-women who simply tell us the things they think we want to hear. Fewer by far are the men and women who will tell us what we *need* to hear. When they do, we're wise to listen—*and to learn.*

Want to do your best? Want to avoid the crater-sized potholes on the road of life? Want to learn things at the school of sound advice instead of the school of hard knocks? Then look for mature friends who are willing to challenge you when necessary. These friends are like diamonds: they're rare *and* valuable.

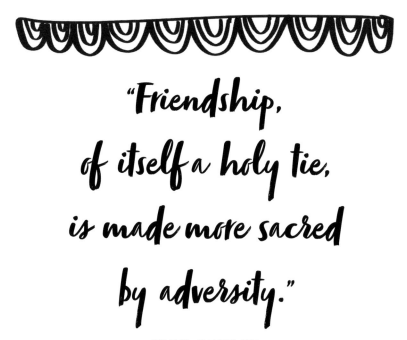

"Friendship, of itself a holy tie, is made more sacred by adversity."

JOHN DRYDEN

Go for the Group

*"Christians are like coals in a fire.
When they cling together, they keep the flame aglow;
when they separate, they die out."*

BILLY GRAHAM

When it comes to studying God's Word, there's strength in numbers. So, if you're not a member of a Bible study group, I strongly recommend that you consider joining one—or organizing one yourself. When friends get together and study God's Word, good things inevitably happen. People grow stronger in their faith, more secure in their knowledge, and more comfortable talking about Jesus. So what's not to like?

When I'm discussing the Bible with friends I can trust, it's a special time for me, a comforting experience to be sure. By hearing different perspectives, I can go deeper into the Word. You can too.

But what if you're *not* a Bible scholar? What if you're a new Christian delving into Scripture for the first time? Does that mean you'll need to keep your mouth tightly closed whenever Bible topics are discussed? Absolutely not! Your perspective is valuable to the group, so don't hesitate to speak up or ask questions.

And what if you're not a "group" person? Personally, I think you should give it a try anyway, even if you're a little bit apprehensive. There's so much good that comes from group Bible studies that it's well worth the time and energy to see if it's right for you.

Speaking of time and energy, I can almost hear you saying, "There's no way I can fit another weekly meeting into my schedule." Okay. I hear what you're saying,

"Our love to God is measured by our everyday fellowship with others and the love it displays."

ANDREW MURRAY

and I feel your stress. But there's no law that says your Bible study group needs to meet every week. Maybe biweekly works best for you, or maybe once a month if you're really swamped. Any group time is better than zero group time. And if you simply cannot find *any* time during the month for a Bible study group, maybe it's time to go back to the beginning of this book and reread the chapter about excuses!

Oil and incense bring joy to the heart, and the sweetness of a friend is better than self-counsel.

PROVERBS 27:9 HCSB

Friends around the World

Never before have we humans had so many opportunities to connect with people around the corner or around the globe. Social media has changed the world, and it's changed the way we make—and keep—good friends. Now, at our fingertips, we can share nonverbal messages of encouragement and hope with friends who need both.

If it weren't for social media, I wouldn't have some of my nearest and dearest friends. Some of you may know Heather Greenwood; she's our creative team leader at Illustrated Faith. We met through an online digital store where a mutual (online) friend connected us, saying we should work together on a project we were both interested in at the time. Little did she know that Heather and I would become quick friends who could learn from—and grow with—each other.

We met before Illustrated Faith was born, so Heather was able to watch as God was doing huge things in our community. It would have been very easy for Heather to just go along for the ride, enjoying the fun moments and being more of an acquaintance than a friend. But Heather became a *true* friend, one who's always there for me in the rough moments, a friend who calls me out if I get ahead of myself and challenges me when I need it. She's the kind of friend who knows what I'm thinking before I even say it, and, to tell you the truth, we've only spent a couple of long weekends together *in person*. But we've spent countless hours texting and in online chats. I'm so thankful that social media connected us! And I'm grateful for so many other life-giving relationships that have enriched my life and strengthened my faith. I have friends and acquaintances all around the globe thanks to all those amazing social networks.

"The best mirror is an old friend."

GEORGE HERBERT

Obviously, social media has its limitations and its drawbacks. But there's no denying that it's changed the way the world communicates. And there's also no denying that it can be a powerful force for good when it's used properly. In fact, social media has become an important tool for sharing our faith and spreading our joy, which, by the way, is the topic of the next chapter.

Your Personal Top 5:
Friendships That Need to Be
Jump-Started

Try to think of five friends you need to reconnect with. Write their names and numbers below. Then pull out the jumper cables.

1. _____

2. _____

3. _____

4. _____

5. _____

As iron sharpens iron,

so people can

improve each other.

PROVERBS 27:17 NCV

Your Personal Top 10: Celebrating Your Friends

On the lines below, make a list of ten friends. Beside each name, write one or two admirable qualities that cause you to admire that person. Then make sure to let each friend know how much you appreciate him or her.

1. _____

2. _____

3. _____

4. _____

5. _____

6. _____

7. _____

8. _____

9. _____

10. _____

A friend loves at all times,
and a brother is born for a time of adversity.
PROVERBS 17:17 NIV

Dear friends, if God loved us in this way,
we also must love one another.
I JOHN 4:11 HCSB

A new commandment I give unto you,
that ye love one another;
as I have loved you, that ye also love one another.
JOHN 13:34 KJV

And now abide faith, hope, love,
these three; but the greatest of these is love.
I CORINTHIANS 13:13 NKJV

#9

Go Out with Great Joy!

"Joy is the great note all throughout the Bible."
OSWALD CHAMBERS

Can we have a little more honesty here? How about some honesty on the topic of joy? Joy is something that we, as Christians, are supposed to possess in huge quantities. But sometimes, here in the real world, joy seems like a rather scarce commodity, at least in my neighborhood.

When the dog eats the homework, or the car won't start, or the computer crashes, or the roof springs a leak, who feels like celebrating? I know I don't. But the more time I spend with God, and the more I fall in love with my Bible, the more I understand that lasting joy has less to do with my circumstances than my faith.

As believers, we have every reason on earth—and in heaven—to be joyful. Even when the storm clouds roll over the horizon and troubles seem to be sprouting like dandelions, we still have so much to be thankful for:

God's love, God's Son, God's creation, and eternal life, for starters. And the list goes on and on and on.

Joyful living is one of those healthy habits that's strengthened by daily Bible reading. In fact, it's one of Bible study's big rewards. We feel better about ourselves and our world when we've been nourished by the Word every day. The Scriptures help us find peace amid the commotion of everyday life, and they help us focus on eternal blessings, not temporary setbacks.

"Fill up the spare moments of your life with praise and thanksgiving."

SARAH YOUNG

Joyful living is a way of thinking, a way of behaving, a way of viewing our surroundings. Joy is a way of relating to our friends, to our families, and to our Creator. Joy is paradoxical: the more of it we give away, the more of it we have. So whenever we go out into the world with great joy, it's a gift to others and to ourselves.

This day, like every other, is a gift from God. When we celebrate it cheerfully, we're blessed. When we worship the Lord with thanks in our hearts and praise on our lips, we're doubly blessed. When we read God's Word and talk to Him often, we experience pockets of joy that serve as reminders of far greater joys to come.

Your life story is being written one day at a time. I pray that it will be a joyful story. And I pray that you'll share your joy with your friends, with your family, and with the world while there's still time.

"The world looks for happiness through self-assertion. The Christian knows that joy is found in self-abandonment."

ELISABETH ELLIOT

"God meant for life to be filled with joy and purpose. He invites us to take our journey with Him."

BILLY GRAHAM

This Is the Day

This is the day the Lord has made;
we will rejoice and be glad in it.

PSALM 118:24 NKJV

When is the best day to go out joyfully and share God's good news with the world? Today sounds good to me. How about you?

Psalm 118:24 reminds us that each day is a cause for rejoicing. This day, like all the ones before it and all the ones that will follow, is a gift from above, a one-of-a-kind treasure, and a cause for celebration.

On those days when all is calm and all is bright, it's easier to celebrate. But what about the other days, the ones that are stormy and dark? On the really tough days, maybe all we can do is hang on, knowing that something better may be just around the corner. And while we're waiting to sing the "happy days are here again" refrain, we can take comfort in the knowledge that, through Jesus, we've achieved the ultimate victory.

"We may run, walk, stumble, drive, or fly, but let us never lose sight of the reason for the journey, or miss a chance to see a rainbow on the way."

GLORIA GAITHER

Read the Word, Share the Word, Share the Joy

"Joy is a by-product not of happy circumstances, education, or talent, but of a healthy relationship with God and a determination to love Him no matter what."

BARBARA JOHNSON

Need a surefire prescription for joy? Here it is: establish a growing, loving, obedient relationship with God and His Word. Read. Pray. Journal. Share. Repeat. When you do, you'll experience more joy, less stress, more peace, and less inner turmoil. And that's good, because the more joy you possess, the more of it you have to share.

Joy is like peanut butter: it's meant to be spread around. But unlike peanut butter, nobody's allergic to joy. So we should be sharing it everywhere we go: at church, at work, at home, at Starbucks, and all points in between.

"Holy activity is the mother of holy joy."

C. H. SPURGEON

So here's another one-month challenge: see how much joy you can generate during the next thirty days. Then see how much of it you can share. The more you share, the more you have; the more you have, the more you share. It's a positive loop that's guaranteed to make *the* world—and *your* world—a better place.

And if you have a bad day, or two, or three, don't

worry. Just keep reading your Bible and praying for God's guidance. When you let Him lead, He will. And when you travel His path, there's more than enough joy to go around.

# # # # # # # # #

"Where the soul is full of peace and joy, outward surroundings and circumstances are of comparatively little account."

HANNAH WHITALL SMITH

# # # # # # # # #

Your Personal Top 5: Where Your Joy Begins

Try to think of five things that bring joy to your heart. (P.S. Is your relationship with Jesus on this list?)

1. _____

2. _____

3. _____

4. _____

5. _____

"A life of intimacy with God is characterized by joy."

OSWALD CHAMBERS

Your Personal Top 10:
Share the Joy

Joy is contagious. On the lines below, make a list of ten people who could probably use a dose of joyfulness right now. The rest is up to you.

1. _____

2. _____

3. _____

4. _____

5. _____

6. _____

7. _____

8. _____

9. _____

10. _____

Rejoice always, pray without ceasing,
in everything give thanks; for this
is the will of God in Christ Jesus for you.
I THESSALONIANS 5:16–18 NKJV

So you also have sorrow now.
But I will see you again. Your hearts will rejoice,
and no one will rob you of your joy.
JOHN 16:22 HCSB

I have spoken these things to you
so that My joy may be in you
and your joy may be complete.
JOHN 15:11 HCSB

I came that they may have life, and have it abundantly.
JOHN 10:10 NASB

#10
Celebrate Your Life

*"If you can forgive the person you were,
accept the person you are, and believe in the person
you will become, you are headed for joy.
So celebrate your life."*

BARBARA JOHNSON

Well, you've made it! You're at chapter 10, and you're still reading. Thank you! As a reward for your perseverance, this final chapter is a tribute to . . . *drumroll please* . . . a truly amazing woman: *you*.

Yes, it's time to celebrate the person you see in the mirror: the woman you *were*, the woman you *are*, and the woman you *will be*. It's time to celebrate your life.

Celebrating is always easier when you're at peace with yourself and your Creator. That's where God's Word comes in. When you fall in love with your Bible and establish a real relationship with its Author, you'll experience pockets of the peace, the same kind of peace that Paul talks about in his letter to the Philippians: "And the peace of God, which transcends all understanding, will guard your hearts and your minds in Christ Jesus" (Philippians 4:7 NIV).

Experiencing peace doesn't mean that everything's

going to be perfect in your life. And it doesn't mean that you'll live a stress-free existence. Life goes on, an entire tapestry of moments, knitted into a pattern that God helps you weave on a loom only He can see.

Some days are almost too *spectacular* for words; other days are almost too *painful* for words. Most days are somewhere in between. So which days should you celebrate? As strange as it seems, the correct answer is, all of them.

All our days are essential elements in God's plan for our lives. Ultimately, He's in charge, and He knows what He's doing. When we acknowledge these facts, we discover the precious peace—His peace—that helps us rise above the challenges of everyday life and celebrate eternal gifts that are, in truth, too beautiful for mere human beings to comprehend.

> "All our life is like a day of celebration to us. We are convinced, in fact, that God is always everywhere."
>
> ST. CLEMENT OF ALEXANDRIA

Falling in love with God's Word binds us to the Creator in a way that we simply can't achieve when we leave our Bibles unread on the shelf. So, for the sake of celebration and peace, let's take a quick review of the ten steps that will help you take that Bible off the shelf and fall in love with it.

> *"The greatest honor you can give Almighty God is to live gladly and joyfully because of the knowledge of His love."*
>
> JULIANA OF NORWICH

#1. Get Rid of the Excuses: Take those tattered excuses for not reading your Bible and toss them all into the trash bin of history—your *personal* history.

#2. Turn the Guilt into a Gift: No more guilty feelings. The Bible is a gift; treat it that way.

#3. Get Personal: Get busy journaling in—and illustrating—your Bible. Use it until it's falling apart.

#4. Write Love Letters to God: He's already written a very long one to you. Now it's your turn.

#5. Get Your *Daily* Dose: Get in touch with God's Word every day. No exceptions. Familiarity breeds contentment.

#6. Be a Fangirl: Get excited. Really excited. And stay that way.

#7. Apply the Lessons: Move beyond the theoretical. God gave us His Word to use it.

#8. Bible, Coffee, and Girlfriends: Find friends who, like you, are determined to fashion a meaningful relationship with the Father and the Son.

#9. Go Out with Great Joy!: Share the good news any way you can, as often as you can, to as many people as you can.

#10. Celebrate Your Life: This day is another gift from above. God loves you, and He created you in His image. These facts are cause for celebration.

"Every day we live is a priceless gift of God, loaded with possibilities to learn something new, to gain fresh insights."

DALE EVANS ROGERS

Celebrate God's Word, God's Gifts, and Yourself

If you've successfully arrived at step #10, you've got plenty to celebrate. You've freed yourself from those pesky excuses and rid yourself of useless guilt. You've personalized your Bible and written letters to your Creator. You're reading your Bible every day, and you're excited about it. But that's not all; you're also applying the lessons you've learned, and sharing your excitement with your friends *and* with the world. Finally, you've made the decision to make every day a cause for some sort of celebration. When you celebrate life, you're showing genuine appreciation to the One who gave you life in the first place.

God made you in His image, and you are His beautiful child, unique throughout all the universe. Your Father has marvelous plans for you, now and throughout eternity. When you consider His blessings and His love, you'll have to agree that there's *always* something good to celebrate. Including the woman in the mirror!

"You are loved, you are beautiful, you are treasured, and you are a daughter of the living God."

SHEILA WALSH

139

And Finally

So many things flood my mind as we wrap up this book. First and foremost, I hope that you will understand that your relationship with Jesus is #1 and that reading your Bible is simply a tool in that relationship. The Bible isn't meant to be worshiped or to be set on the shelf as a shrine, but rather to be a tool in your tool belt, to live life with you.

Instead of my Bible sitting on the shelf collecting dust, it is now peeking out of my purse at the store or sitting on the car seat when I pick up the kids from play practice. It sits open on my desk throughout the day; it's always there, an open invitation to learn more, to grow more, to dig deeper into my relationship with my Father.

It's my hope that through these ten steps, you, too, will celebrate this journey. And I pray that you'll discover that same never-ending delight in His Word!

You will teach me how to live a holy life. Being with you will fill me with joy; at your right hand I will find pleasure forever.

PSALM 16:11 NCV

Rejoice always, pray without ceasing,
in everything give thanks;
for this is the will of God in Christ Jesus for you.
I THESSALONIANS 5:16–18 NKJV

A joyful heart is good medicine,
but a broken spirit dries up the bones.
PROVERBS 17:22 HCSB

Rejoice and be exceedingly glad,
for great is your reward in heaven.
MATTHEW 5:12 NKJV

Until now you have asked for nothing in My name.
Ask and you will receive,
that your joy may be complete.
JOHN 16:24 HCSB

The End

30-Day Journaling Challenge

Day 1

Day 2

Day 3

Day 4

Day 5

Day 6

Day 7

Day 8

Day 9

Day 10

Day 11

Day 12

Day 13

Day 14

Day 15

Day 16

Day 17

Day 18

Day 19

Day 20

Day 21

Day 22

Day 23

Day 24

Day 25

Day 26

Day 27

Day 28

Day 29

Day 30

30 Days of Joy

Day 1

Day 2

Day 3

Day 4

Day 5

Day 6

Day 7

Day 8

Day 9

Day 10

Day 11

Day 12

Day 13

Day 14

Day 15

Day 16

Day 17

Day 18

Day 19

Day 20

Day 21

Day 22

Day 23

Day 24

Day 25

Day 26

Day 27

Day 28

Day 29

Day 30

About the Author

Shanna Noel lives in Washington State with her husband of eighteen years, Jonathan, and their two daughters, Jaden (15) and Addison (10). When they aren't covered in paint and Bible journaling, they are working on reclaimed projects around the house or catching up on the latest movie.

Shanna is the founder and owner of Illustrated Faith and the Bible-journaling community, and stands in awe at what God is doing in their creative community!

you are loved
+ + + + + + + + + + + + + + + + + +
fall in love with your life
♡ ♡ ♡ ♡ ♡ ♡ ♡ ♡ ♡ ♡ ♡
tis word is for you
+ + + + + + + + + + + + + + +
you are loved
+ + + + + + + + + + + + + + + + +
fall in love with your life
♡ ♡ ♡ ♡ ♡ ♡ ♡ ♡ ♡ ♡ ♡
tis word is for you
+ + + + + + + + + + + + + + +
you are loved
+ + + + + + + + + + + + + + + +
fall in love with your life
♡ ♡ ♡ ♡ ♡ ♡ ♡ ♡ ♡ ♡
tis word is for you
+ + + + + + + + + + + + + + +
you are loved

LIVE YOUR FAITH

Dear Friend,

This book was prayerfully crafted with you, the reader, in mind—every word, every sentence, every page—was thoughtfully written, designed, and packaged to encourage you...right where you are this very moment. At DaySpring, our vision is to see every person experience the life-changing message of God's love. So, as we worked through rough drafts, design changes, edits, and details, we prayed for you to deeply experience His unfailing love, indescribable peace, and pure joy. It is our sincere hope that through these Truth-filled pages your heart will be blessed, knowing that God cares about you—your desires and disappointments, your challenges and dreams.

He knows. He cares. He loves you unconditionally.

BLESSINGS!
THE DAYSPRING BOOK TEAM

Additional copies of this book and other DaySpring titles can be purchased at fine bookstores everywhere.
Order online at dayspring.com
or
by phone at 1-877-751-4347